Microwave

COOKING

Microwave cooking is fun, quick and easy

Cooking this way generally preserves vitamins and minerals and also brings out the full taste of the ingredients used – dishes really taste of all the good things that have gone into them.

Try these delicious and nutritious recipes for yourself and discover the advantages of 'fast wave' cooking. However, do take note of the important advice on page 64.

AURA

CONTENTS

What are microwaves?

Like radio and television waves, microwaves are electro-magnetic waves. Using a microwave oven differs from conventional cooking methods in that the food is cooked directly by microwaves without its container interfering with and absorbing the heat. Microwaves can penetrate glass, earthenware, china and synthetic materials without loss of energy, going straight into the food being cooked. They cause the fat, water and sugar molecules in the food to vibrate rapidly and as these molecules rub against each other, heat is generated and the food cooks. As water molecules vibrate the most, a microwave is especially suitable for cooking all moist foods.

The only really important exception is any kind of metal, which should never be used in a microwave oven because the electromagnetic waves are reflected off the metal and so cannot reach the food. Further, this can result in irreparable damage to the magnetron, which generates the microwaves, ruining a perfectly good kitchen appliance.

Choosing your microwave

Your choice of oven depends chiefly on what you want to use it for and, to some extent, on the number of people in the family. According to your requirements, you can select a standard or a combination model. Microwave ovens also range from very basic designs to highly sophisticated models with numerous extra features. They also vary in their power output.

Microwave ovens are fitted with a temperature/power control. Many modern microwaves have a maximum output of 800–1,000 watts for rapid heating of food and liquids. However, this is too powerful for cooking. They are generally more suitable for commercial than domestic use. An output of 500–720 watts (HIGH) is quite sufficient for this. More delicate ingredients need to be cooked at 300–490 watts (MEDIUM) and 180 watts (LOW) is high enough for food requiring slower, longer cooking.

Microwave ovens with a maximum output of 400 watts are also available. These are mainly suitable for warming up ready-cooked dishes and, of course, for defrosting frozen food. They are less suitable for cooking raw ingredients because their low wattage makes the cooking time too long. All microwaves have a defrost setting.

Combination microwaves

Combination ovens can be used for microwaving and other, conventional cooking , such as grilling and browning. With these ovens you can cook such things as cakes and gratins, which not only need to be cooked quickly, but also browned on top.

Some combination ovens are fitted with fixed cooking programmes, so you are not free to set the wattage and temperature yourself. Information about these fixed programmes is to be found in the manufacturer's instructions.

Microwave containers

Of course you do not have to buy a completely new set of crockery and kitchen ware for the microwave. You can use many of the bowls and dishes you already have: glass, china (without gold or silver decoration) and earthenware plates, dishes and bowls are nearly always suitable. If you are uncertain whether a container is suitable, do the crockery test (see below).

In fact, you can use a much wider variety of containers in a microwave oven than you can for conventional cooking. These include kitchen paper, paper napkins, greaseproof paper and paper plates, as well as suitable plastics (see page 6)

Crockery test
Put the dish half filled with water into the microwave oven and heat on HIGH for 30 seconds. If it remains cold or just slightly warm and the water is heating up, it is quite safe to use. Any dishes that become hot are not suitable for use in the microwave oven.

Terrines, bowls, dishes and plates can all be used in the microwave – provided they are made of glass, china, earthenware or the right sort of plastic.

Glass

Microwaves can pass through glass without losing energy. This shortens the cooking time. An additional advantage is that you can keep an eye on the cooking process.

However, do not use very thin glass or glass with even the smallest crack in it because it could break during cooking or when you take it out of the oven, causing injury.

Pottery, stoneware and earthenware

These are all well suited to the microwave provided they do not have a metal glaze or decoration. The glaze should cover the dish smoothly, otherwise cracks could appear. It is recommended that you do the crockery test on dishes that are not marked as suitable for a microwave oven.

Plastic materials

Containers made from synthetic materials have been especially developed for microwave cookery, but these are not really for combination ovens, which can cause them to melt. A great advantage of plastic containers is that food can be frozen, thawed and cooked in them. A good guide to the suitability of plastic containers is that they are dishwasher-safe. Do not use melamine, and most plastics are unsuitable for foods with a high fat or sugar content.

China

China without any metal decoration or glaze is well suited to standard microwaves. Never use crockery with gilt rims, as the electromagnetic waves would be reflected off the metal parts. They might even spark or the decoration may blacken and be permanently damaged. Use only ovenproof china in combination microwave appliances and always follow the manufacturer's advice.

Baking tins

As a nice brown topping is usually required when baking, you can do this only in a combination microwave oven. You can get good results with utensils made out of black tin or coated with black tin. As it conducts heat well, the food you are baking will turn crispy brown during the short baking time. Be very careful that the baking tin does not come into contact with the sides of the microwave oven. Microwave-safe baking tins are specially manufactured.

Microwave clear film

This is very useful for covering food when the container has no lid. Pierce the wrap several time with a fork to allow the steam to escape.

Do not use ordinary plastic wrap that is designed for storage only. The heat can affect its chemical constituent, releasing potentially dangerous substances.

Various microwave-safe plastic pouches and roasting bags are available from most supermarkets.

Aluminium foil

As it is made of metal, foil does not let microwaves through it. You can make good use of this fact when, for example, you are cooking meat on the bone. You can cover the ends of protruding bones with small pieces of foil to prevent them charring. However, you should never use large pieces of aluminium foil. Greaseproof paper is often a good substitute.

Useful tips

Warming food

Many families find it impossible to eat together on weekdays. Cooked meals can be easily warmed up in single portions. Warm the food on a plate in the microwave oven on HIGH for 2 minutes. Covering the plate with microwave clear film will prevent the top from becoming too dry.

Vegetables in their jackets

If you cook vegetables, such as potatoes, tomatoes and whole green peppers in their skins, you must pierce them several times with a fork before cooking. Otherwise the skin will burst under pressure from inside. You should never cook eggs in their shells in a microwave, and before cooking fried eggs, carefully pierce the yolk with a cocktail stick.

Blanching almonds

Put the almonds in hot water in a bowl and cook on HIGH. 115 g/4 oz almonds need about 1 minute. Then rinse the

Stuffed tomatoes

Good value • Quick

Instead of halloumi cheese you can use mozzarella. If you have a combination microwave oven, cook the tomatoes on MEDIUM with the grill switched on for about 10 minutes, until they are well browned on top.

Serves 2
2 medium tomatoes
  (about 200 g/7 oz)
½ bunch fresh basil
½ bunch fresh parsley
1 garlic clove
50 g/2 oz halloumi cheese
7.5 ml/1½ teaspoons olive oil
salt
freshly ground black pepper
pinch of sugar
fresh basil sprigs, to garnish

Approximately per portion:
440 kj/100 kcal
5 g protein
8 g fat
4 g carbohydrate

● Approximate preparation
  time: 20 minutes
---

1. Cut the tomatoes in half crossways. Scoop out the flesh with a teaspoon, taking care not to damage the 'shell', and chop finely. Pull the the basil and parsley leaves off the stems and finely chop. Crush the garlic. Cut the cheese into small cubes.

2. Mix together the tomato flesh, basil, parsley, garlic, cheese and

olive oil. Season to taste with salt, pepper and sugar.

3. Fill the scooped-out tomatoes with the mixture, using a teaspoon.

4. Arrange the tomatoes evenly spaced on a microwave-proof plate and cook on HIGH for about 6 minutes, until the cheese has completely melted. Serve the tomatoes hot or warm, garnished with fresh basil sprigs.

Tip

Halloumi is a Greek cheese, usually made from ewe's milk. It has a creamy texture and a slightly salty taste. It is particularly useful for cooking and should be eaten while it is still hot, as it goes very rubbery if allowed to cool down. Rinse with milk or water before using.

Stuffed mushrooms with gorgonzola

Vegetarian

Mushrooms are also very successful in combination microwave ovens. They take 11 minutes on MEDIUM under a medium grill.

Serves 4
400 g/14 oz large button
  mushrooms
50 g/2 oz shelled pistachio nuts
50 g/2 oz gorgonzola cheese

1 small tomato
½ bunch fresh parsley
salt
freshly ground white pepper
fresh parsley sprigs, to garnish

Approximately per portion:
590 kj/140 kcal
8 g protein
11 g fat
3 g carbohydrate

● Approximate preparation
  time: 30 minutes
---

1. Remove the stalks from the mushrooms and chop finely. Finely chop the pistachio nuts. Crumble or dice the gorgonzola cheese. Skin and dice the tomato. Finely chop the parsley.

2. Mix together the chopped mushroom stalks, pistachio nuts, cheese and parsley and season to taste with salt and pepper. Pile the mixture into the mushroom caps.

3. Arrange the mushrooms evenly spaced in a microwave-proof dish and cook on HIGH for about 8 minutes, until the cheese has melted. Serve the mushrooms hot or cold, garnished with fresh parsley sprigs.

Above: Stuffed mushrooms with gorgonzola
Below: Stuffed tomatoes

Fennel timbales with horseradish sauce

Exquisite

Instead of fennel you can use beetroot or carrots for the timbales. If you cannot obtain fresh horseradish, substitute 10 ml/ 2 teaspoons creamed horseradish.

Serves 4
300 g/11 oz fennel bulbs
90 ml/6 tablespoons water
20 g/¾ oz chilled butter, plus extra
*   for greasing*
1 egg
1 egg yolk
50 ml/2 fl oz chilled double cream
salt
freshly ground black pepper
grated rind from 1 lemon
1 small horseradish root
½ tart apple
1 bunch fresh chives
150 ml/¼ pint soured cream
15 ml/1 tablespoon crème fraîche

Approximately per portion:
1,200 kj/290 kcal
7 g protein
24 g fat
8 g carbohydrate

● Approximate preparation
   time: 1 hour

1. Cut the fennel bulbs into quarters and cut out the stalks. Reserve the feathery fronds. Slice the fennel quarters into thin strips.

2. Put the fennel strips and water in a microwave-proof bowl, cover and cook on HIGH for about 8 minutes, stirring once.

3. Meanwhile, finely chop the reserved fennel tops. Drain the cooked fennel and refresh under cold running water, drain and set aside to cool.

4. Put the cold fennel and the butter in a food processor and work to a smooth purée. Transfer the mixture to a bowl. Stir in the egg, egg yolk and cream and mix well. Season with salt and pepper and stir in lemon rind to taste. Finally, stir in the fennel tops.

5. Thoroughly grease 4 small (175 ml/6 fl oz) microwave-proof pudding bowls or dariole moulds with butter. Fill them with the fennel mixture and cover them with microwave clear film. Pierce the cover several times with a needle so that the steam can escape during cooking.

6. To make the sauce, peel a section of the horseradish root and finely grate about 1 cm/ ½ inch. Peel and finely grate the apple. Snip the chives.

Variation

If you have difficulty in obtaining horseradish, a simple herb crème fraîche is a tasty substitute. Mix together crème fraîche, lemon juice and mustard. Stir in about 15 ml/1 tablespoon chopped, fresh mixed herbs. Season the sauce with salt, freshly ground white pepper and 1 crushed garlic clove, if liked. Store in the refrigerator until ready to be served.

7. Mix together the horseradish, apple, chives, soured cream and crème fraîche. Season to taste with salt and pepper.

8. Arrange the bowls or dariole moulds in a circle in the microwave and cook the puddings on MEDIUM for about 7 minutes, until the mixture thickens. Carefully tip the timbales out on to individual plates and serve with the horseradish sauce.

Cream of tomato soup with herbs

Easy to make

If you want to vary this soup, you could add prawns or a small, chopped white fish fillet, such as plaice or whiting, with the crème fraîche. Then heat for a further 2 minutes on HIGH.

Serves 2
500 g/1¼ lb tomatoes
1 shallot
1 garlic clove
1 bunch fresh thyme
1 bunch fresh parsley
6 fresh marjoram leaves
7.5 ml/1½ teaspoons olive oil
120 ml/4 fl oz chicken or
  vegetable stock
salt
freshly ground white pepper
pinch of sugar
15–30 ml/1–2 tablespoons crème
  fraîche

Approximately per portion:
420 kj/100 kcal
4 g protein
5 g fat
10 g carbohydrate

● Approximate preparation
  time: 35 minutes

---

1. Blanch the tomatoes in boiling water for 1–2 minutes, drain and rinse with cold water. Skin and dice the tomato flesh. Finely chop the shallot and garlic. Strip the thyme leaves from their stems. Remove any thick stems from the parsley and finely chop the leaves. Finely chop the marjoram leaves.

2. Put the shallot, garlic and olive oil into a microwave-proof bowl. Cook on HIGH for 1 minute.

3. Add the tomatoes, chicken or vegetable stock, thyme, parsley and marjoram. Season to taste with salt and pepper and stir in the sugar. Cover and cook on HIGH for about 6 minutes.

4. Adjust the seasoning if necessary. Stir in the crème fraîche. Pour the tomato soup immediately into warmed individual bowls and serve hot.

Asparagus soup

Easy to make

Serves 3
500 g/1¼ lb white asparagus
400 ml/14 fl oz water
salt
pinch of sugar
½ bunch fresh chervil
30 ml/2 tablespoons double cream
freshly ground white pepper
croûtons, to serve (optional)

Approximately per portion:
110 kj/26 kcal
3 g protein
2 g fat
3 g carbohydrate

● Approximate preparation
  time: 30 minutes

---

1. Trim the woody ends of the asparagus stalks and peel from top to bottom. Cut off and reserve the tips. Cut the stems into pieces.

2. Put the asparagus stems, water and salt and sugar to taste into a microwave-proof bowl and stir to mix. Cover and cook on HIGH for about 8 minutes.

3. Add the asparagus tips and cook on HIGH for a further 6 minutes, or until the asparagus stems are tender.

4. Meanwhile, finely chop the chervil and set aside.

5. Remove and reserve the asparagus tips from the bowl. Put the remaining mixture into a food processor or blender and work to make a smooth purée. Return the mixture to the bowl. Gently stir in the cream and asparagus tips. Season the soup with salt and pepper to taste. Cover and cook on HIGH for a further 2 minutes.

6. Ladle the soup into 3 individual soup bowls, sprinkle over the chervil and serve immediately, with croûtons, if liked.

Tip

To make croûtons, cut the crusts off 1 slice bread and cut the bread into small cubes. Fry lightly in butter or olive oil until golden brown and crisp.

Above: Asparagus soup
Below: Cream of tomato soup with herbs

Potato and leek soup

Good value

It is best to use a floury variety of potato, such as King Edward or Maris Piper. This makes the soup nice and thick.

Serves 2–3
300 g/11 oz potatoes
200 g/7 oz leeks
15 g/½ oz butter
300 ml/½ pint vegetable or
*   chicken stock*
45 ml/3 tablespoons double cream
salt
freshly ground white pepper
pinch of grated nutmeg
½ bunch chives

For 2 people approximately per portion:
950 kj/230 kcal
6 g protein
10 g fat
27 g carbohydrate

● Approximate preparation
   time: 35 minutes

---

1. Dice the potatoes. Thinly slice the leeks. Dice the butter.

2. Put the potatoes, leeks and butter into a microwave-proof bowl and cook on HIGH for 2 minutes.

3. Stir in the vegetable or chicken stock and the cream. Season to taste with salt and pepper and stir in the nutmeg. Cover and cook on HIGH, stirring once or twice, for 12 minutes, until the potatoes are cooked through and soft.

4. Meanwhile, snip the chives.

5. Serve the soup in individual bowls, garnished with chives.

Variation
You can substitute courgettes for the leeks. Dice finely and cook in the same way.

Hot pepper soup

Easy to make

Serves 2
1 small red pepper
*   (about 150 g/5 oz)*
1 small green pepper
*   (about 150 g/5 oz)*
1 small yellow pepper
*   (about 150 g/5 oz)*
1 onion
1 garlic clove
7.5 ml/1½ teaspoons olive oil
500 ml/17 fl oz vegetable or
*   chicken stock*
salt
2.5 ml/1½ teaspoons hot paprika
7.5 ml/1½ teaspoons mild paprika
30 ml/2 tablespoons soured cream,
*   to garnish*

Approximately per portion:
490 kj/120 kcal
5 g protein
6 g fat
11 g carbohydrate

● Approximate preparation
   time: 40 minutes

---

1. Core and the peppers and cut the flesh into strips. Finely chop the onion and garlic.

2. Put the onion, garlic and olive oil into a microwave-proof bowl and cook on HIGH for 1 minute.

3. Add the peppers and vegetable or chicken stock. Cover and cook on HIGH for about 7 minutes, until the peppers are tender, but still firm to the bite.

4. Season the soup with salt to taste and stir in the hot and mild paprika. Pour the soup into warmed individual bowls, garnish each with 15 ml/1 tablespoon soured cream and serve at once.

Tip

Both mild and hot peppers are used to make paprika, so check the labels carefully. However, even hot paprika is much milder and sweeter than cayenne pepper and chilli powder.

Above: Potato and leek soup
Below: Hot pepper soup

Haddock with lemon butter

Quick • Good value

Instead of haddock you can use plaice, lemon sole, dab or monkfish fillets.

Serves 3
600 g/1 lb 5 oz haddock
  fillets
1 lemon
salt
freshly ground white pepper
1 bunch fresh dill
1 bunch fresh chives
65 g/2½ oz softened butter
boiled new potatoes and mixed
  salad, to serve

Approximately per portion:
1,600 kj/380 kcal
37 g protein
24 g fat
3 g carbohydrate

● Approximate preparation
  time: 20 minutes

---

1. Cut each fish fillet in half lengthways using a sharp, flexible knife, so that you have 2 thin slices from each fillet.

2. Peel the lemon and remove as much of the white pith as possible, using a sharp knife. Cut the lemon into small dice.

3. Season the fish fillets with salt and pepper to taste. Remove any thick stalks from the dill and very finely chop or snip the leaves. Snip the chives.

4. Cream the butter with a fork and beat in the dill, chives and diced lemon.

5. Arrange the fish slices side by side in a single layer in a large microwave-proof dish. Dot them with the lemon butter.

6. Cover and cook on HIGH for about 5½ minutes. Transfer the fish to individual warmed plates and serve immediately with boiled new potatoes and mixed salad.

Variation
You can substitute 2 small limes for the lemon or, for a sweeter flavour, you could use a small orange.

Salmon in tomato sauce

Exquisite • Easy to make

Serves 2–3
400 g/14 oz salmon fillets
juice of ½ small lemon
300 g/11 oz tomatoes
1 bunch fresh basil
105 ml/7 tablespoons crème fraîche
salt
freshly ground white pepper
fresh basil sprigs and fresh dill
  sprigs, to garnish

For 2 people approximately per portion:
1,700 kj/400 kcal
29 g protein
29 g fat
5 g carbohydrate

● Approximate preparation
  time: 30 minutes

---

1. Remove any remaining bones from the salmon with tweezers. Then cut the fish into bite-size pieces. Put them in a bowl, gently stir in the lemon juice and set aside in the refrigerator.

2. Blanch the tomatoes in boiling water for 1–2 minutes. Drain, rinse in cold water and skin them. Cut the tomato flesh into very small dice. Pull the fresh basil leaves off their stalks and cut them into very thin strips.

3. Mix together the crème fraîche, tomatoes and basil and season well with salt and pepper.

4. Season the salmon with salt and pepper to taste and put it into a microwave-proof dish.

5. Pour over the tomato sauce. Cover and cook on HIGH for about 5 minutes, stirring gently once. Transfer the salmon with the tomato sauce to individual warmed plates and serve, garnished with basil and dill sprigs.

Above: Haddock with lemon butter
Below: Salmon in tomato sauce

Plaice with mustard sauce

Exquisite

Serves 4
105 ml/7 tablespoons crème fraîche
105 ml/7 tablespoons double cream
10 ml/2 teaspoons Dijon mustard
pinch of English mustard powder
15 ml/1 tablespoon dry sherry
salt
freshly ground white pepper
8 x 90 g/3½ oz plaice fillets
7.5 ml/1½ teaspoons lemon juice
1 bunch fresh parsley
tomato rice or boiled new potatoes,
*   to serve*

Approximately per portion:
1,200 kj/290 kcal
29 g protein
17 g fat
2 g carbohydrate

● Approximate preparation
   time: 30 minutes

---

1. Using a wire whisk, beat together the crème fraîche, double cream, Dijon mustard, mustard powder and sherry with salt and pepper to taste.

2. Arrange the plaice fillets in a single layer in a large microwave-proof dish.

3. Sprinkle over the lemon juice. Spread the mustard sauce evenly over the fish.

4. Cover and cook on HIGH for about 5 minutes. Halfway through the cooking time, carefully move the fillets on the outside of the dish to the centre and and those in the centre to the outside.

5. Meanwhile, pull the parsley leaves off the stems and chop them finely.

6. Transfer the plaice fillets, together with the mustard sauce, to individual warmed plates. Sprinkle over the parsley and serve immediately with tomato rice or boiled new potatoes.

Prawns in herb cream

Quick to make

Serves 2–3
400 g/14 oz raw prawns
15 ml/1 tablespoon lemon juice
1 shallot
½ bunch fresh dill
½ bunch fresh parsley
2 sprigs fresh lemon balm
150 ml/¼ pint double cream
salt
freshly ground white pepper
boiled rice, to serve

For 2 people approximately per portion:
1,700 kj/400 kcal
40 g protein, 27 g fat
5 g carbohydrate

● Approximate preparation
   time: about 20 minutes

---

1. Remove the heads and peel and devein the prawns, leaving the tails intact. Put them in a dish, sprinkle over the lemon juice, cover and set aside in the refrigerator.

2. Finely chop the shallot. Remove the thick stems from the dill, parsley and lemon balm and finely chop the leaves.

3. Put the shallot, dill, parsley, lemon balm and cream in a microwave-proof dish and season with salt and pepper to taste.

4. Cook the sauce on HIGH for about 3 minutes.

5. Stir the prawns into the sauce, cover and cook on HIGH, stirring once, for about 3 minutes, until they change colour. Transfer the prawns to individual serving plates and spoon over the sauce. Serve immediately with boiled rice.

Tip

Cooking times for the recipes are given only as a guide and should not to be followed to the second. Appliances of the same wattage often produce different results and older appliances may take a little longer. This means that you may have to cook many dishes a little longer. You will be the best judge once you are familiar with your own microwave.

Above: Plaice with mustard sauce
Below: Prawns in herb cream

Monkfish with spinach

Exquisite • Easy to make

Serves 2
300 g/11 oz spinach
1 small onion
1 garlic clove
15 g/½ oz butter
75 ml/5 tablespoons double cream
salt
freshly ground white pepper
2 x 185 g/6½ oz monkfish fillets
1 tablespoon lemon juice
45 ml/3 tablespoons finely chopped
   fresh parsley or coriander,
   to garnish
boiled new potatoes, to serve

Approximately per portion:
1,400 kj/330 kcal
31 g protein
19 g fat
6 g carbohydrate

● Approximate preparation
   time: 30 minutes

---

1. Remove and discard any tough or withered leaves and thick stalks from the spinach, then chop the leaves coarsely. Finely chop the onion and garlic.

2. Mix together the onion, garlic and butter in a microwave-proof dish. Cook on HIGH for about 2 minutes.

3. Add the cream and the spinach and season to taste with salt and pepper. Cover and cook on HIGH, stirring once, for about 4 minutes, until the spinach has wilted and broken up.

4. Sprinkle the monkfish fillets with the lemon juice and season with salt and pepper to taste.

5. Arrange the monkfish fillets on top of the spinach. Cover and cook on HIGH for about 6 minutes.

6. Divide the monkfish and spinach between 2 individual warmed serving plates. Garnish with the chopped fresh parsley and serve with boiled new potatoes.

Cod with root vegetables

Good value • Easy to make

You can use any robust white fish for this dish.

Serves 4
4 x 200 g/7 oz cod steaks
juice of 1 small lemon
150 g/5 oz carrots
150 g/5 oz celery
1 leek
1 bunch fresh parsley
15 ml/1 tablespoon water
50 ml/2 fl oz dry white wine
salt
freshly ground white pepper
1 bunch fresh dill
mashed potatoes, to serve

Approximately per portion:
790 kj/190 kcal
37 g protein
1 g fat
6 g carbohydrate

● Approximate preparation
   time: 45 minutes

---

1. Place the cod steaks in a shallow dish and sprinkle over the lemon juice. Set aside.

2. Finely dice the carrots and celery. Thinly slice the leek. Remove any thick stalks from the parsley and finely chop the leaves.

3. Put the carrots, celery, leek parsley and water into a microwave-proof dish. Cover and cook on HIGH, stirring once, for about 4 minutes.

4. Pour in the wine and season the vegetables with salt and pepper to taste. Season the cod with salt and pepper to taste and arrange it on top of the vegetables.

5. Cover and cook the cod on MEDIUM, turning once, for about 10 minutes.

6. Meanwhile, remove the thick stalks and finely chop the dill. Transfer the cod steaks to individual warmed serving plates, sprinkle over the dill and spoon over the vegetables. Serve with mashed potatoes.

Tip

Steaks are cut from the tail end of round fish and cutlets are cut from the centre.

Above: Monkfish with spinach
Below: Cod with root vegetables

Quenelles in dill sauce

Exquisite •
Rather time-consuming

The name comes from the German, *Knödel*, meaning dumpling, but quenelles are, in fact, a speciality from the Lyon region of France. They are traditionally made with pike or zander fillet, but as this can be difficult to obtain, you can substitute salmon. Veal and chicken quenelles are made in the same way.

Serves 3
400 g/14 oz pike, zander or
* salmon fillets*
2 slices bread
1 shallot
1 garlic clove
½ lemon
1 egg
salt
freshly ground white pepper
1 bunch fresh dill
250 ml/8 fl oz double cream
30 ml/2 tablespoon dry white wine
boiled rice, to serve

Approximately per portion:
1,800 kj/430 kcal
33 g protein
27 g fat
11 g carbohydrate

● Approximate preparation
  time: 50 minutes

1. Cut the fish fillets into small cubes. Remove the crusts and dice the bread. Coarsely chop the shallot. Coarsely chop the garlic. Finely grate the lemon rind and then squeeze out the lemon juice.

2. Put the fish, bread, shallot and garlic in a food processor and work to make a smooth purée. Alternatively, grind the fish, bread, shallot and garlic in a mincer. Transfer the purée to a mixing bowl. Add the egg, season with salt and pepper to taste and mix in the lemon rind and about 15 ml/ 1 tablespoon of the lemon juice.

3. Mix thoroughly, then form the mixture into walnut-sized balls between the palms of your hands.

4. Arrange the quenelles on a microwave-proof plate and cover with microwave clear film. Pierce the film several times with a needle to allow the steam to escape during cooking.

5. Remove the thick stalks from the dill and finely chop the leaves. Reserve about one-quarter of the dill for the garnish.

Tip

To test the seasoning, form a small quantity of the mixture into a quenelle and cook it on HIGH for about 20 seconds. Alternative herbs for flavouring the quenelles are chopped fresh tarragon and chervil.

6. Mix together the cream, white wine and remaining dill in a microwave-proof dish and season to taste with salt and pepper. Cover and cook the sauce on HIGH for 2 minutes. Remove the dish from the microwave oven and set aside, still covered.

7. Cook the quenelles on HIGH for about 3 minutes.

8. Transfer the quenelles to the dish of sauce, cover and cook on HIGH for a further 1 minute. Divide the quenelles and sauce between 3 individual, warmed plates. Serve immediately, garnished with the remaining dill and with boiled rice.

Meatballs with fennel

Good value

Serves 2
1 small red onion
½ bunch fresh parsley
200 g/7 oz minced beef
1 egg, lightly beaten
salt
freshly ground black pepper
1 fennel bulb (about 400 g/14 oz)
10 g/¼ oz butter, diced
30 ml/2 tablespoons water
15 ml/1 tablespoon crème fraîche
mashed potatoes (optional), to serve

Approximately per portion:
1,800 kj/430 kcal
34 g protein
26 g fat
14 g carbohydrate

● Approximate preparation
  time: 40 minutes

1. Finely chop the onion. Remove the thick stalks from the parsley and finely chop the leaves.

2. Mix together the minced beef, onion, parsley and egg and season to taste with salt and pepper. Break off small pieces of the mixture and form into walnut-sized balls with the palms of your hands. Place the meatballs on a plate, cover and set aside.

3. Trim the fennel and reserve the fine fronds. Cut the fennel bulb into quarters and then into matchstick strips. Finely chop the fennel fronds.

4. Put the fennel, the chopped fronds and the butter in a microwave-proof dish and cook on HIGH for about 2 minutes.

5. Add the water and season the fennel with salt and pepper to taste. Cover and cook the fennel on HIGH, stirring once, for about 6 minutes, until tender but firm to the bite.

6. Stir the crème fraîche into the fennel. Arrange the meatballs on the vegetables. Cover and cook on HIGH for about 4 minutes, until they are evenly coloured. Serve immediately with mashed potatoes, if liked.

Tip

When buying fennel, look for well-rounded bulbs without bruises or broken leaves. Flat bulbs are immature and lack flavour. Bulbs may be elongated or squat in shape.

Lamb curry with beans

Exquisite

Serves 2
300 g/11 oz green beans
1 small onion
1 garlic clove
½ bunch fresh savory
150 g/5 oz boneless leg of lamb
10 g/¼ oz butter
30 ml/2 tablespoons water
15 ml/1 tablespoon crème fraîche
45–60 ml/3–4 tablespoons dry
  white wine
salt
2.5 ml/½ teaspoon turmeric
1.5 ml/¼ teaspoon cayenne pepper
1.5 ml/¼ teaspoon ground cumin
1.5 ml/¼ teaspoon ground coriander
1.5 ml/¼ teaspoon ground ginger
fresh savory sprigs, to garnish
boiled rice, to serve

Approximately per portion:
1,300 kj/310 kcal
18 g protein
19 g fat
12 g carbohydrate

● Approximate preparation
  time: 40 minutes

1. Top and tail the beans and break the larger ones into 2–3 pieces. Finely chop the onion and garlic. Pull the fresh savory leaves off the stalks.

2. Trim the fat from the lamb and cut the flesh into small strips.

3. Put the beans, savory, onion, garlic and butter into a microwave-proof dish. Cook on HIGH for about 2 minutes.

4. Add the water, cover and cook on HIGH, stirring once, for about 8 minutes, until the beans are tender but still firm to the bite.

5. Add the crème fraîche, wine and lamb and season with salt. Stir in the turmeric, cayenne pepper, cumin, coriander and ginger. Cover and cook on HIGH, stirring once, for 4 minutes. Garnish with savory sprigs and serve with boiled rice.

Above: Meatballs with fennel
Below: Lamb curry with beans

Chicken fricassée with vegetables

Good value

You can also use turkey breast or veal for this fricassée. Dice the meat and cook in the microwave in the same way.

Serves 3
115 g/4 oz button mushrooms
1 red pepper
200 g/7 oz shelled peas
* (fresh or frozen)*
15 g/½ oz butter, diced
700 g/1½ lb boneless chicken
* breasts*
7.3 ml/1½ teaspoons flour
120 ml/4 fl oz chicken stock
120 ml/4 fl oz double cream
salt
freshly ground white pepper
1 egg yolk
15–30 ml/1–2 tablespoons lemon
* juice*
15–30 ml/1–2 teaspoons capers
boiled risotto rice, to serve

> **Approximately per portion:**
> 1,500 kj/360 kcal
> 33 g protein
> 19 g fat
> 11 g carbohydrate
>
> ● Approximate preparation
>   time: 40 minutes

1. Cut the mushrooms into quarters. Seed, core and halve the red pepper. Then cut the flesh into matchstick strips.

2. Put the mushrooms, red pepper strips, peas and butter into a microwave-proof dish.

3. Cook on HIGH, stirring once, for about 4 minutes. Meanwhile, remove and discard the skin from the chicken breasts and cut the flesh into bite-size pieces.

4. Stir the flour into the vegetables until it is completely incorporated and cook on HIGH for about 1 minute.

5. Stir in the chicken stock and cream. Mix thoroughly. Season to taste with salt and pepper and cook on HIGH, stirring once. for about 4 minutes, boiling to reduce the liquid.

6. Add the chicken pieces to the dish. Cover and cook on HIGH, stirring once, for about 4 minutes, until the meat turns an even colour.

7. Meanwhile, beat the egg yolk with the lemon juice. Stir it into the chicken fricassée, together with the capers. Cook on LOW for about 30 seconds.

---

8. Taste and, if necessary, add more salt and pepper. Transfer to individual warmed plates and serve with risotto rice.

Tip

Food stays hot longer if it is served on warmed plates. It is very easy to do this: sprinkle a few drops of water on the plates and heat them in the microwave on HIGH for about 1 minute.

Not just a delight to the palate, tender chicken with aromatically cooked vegetables is also a feast to the eyes.

Turkey ragoût with tomatoes and courgettes

Easy to make

Serves 3
300 g/11 oz boneless turkey
salt
freshly ground black pepper
1 red onion
1 garlic clove
1 courgette
300 g/11 oz tomatoes
½ bunch fresh basil
15 ml/1 tablespoon crème fraîche
boiled rice, to serve

Approximately per portion:
650 kj/150 kcal
23 g protein
4 g fat
6 g carbohydrate

● Approximate preparation
  time: 30 minutes

---

1. Cut the turkey into bite-size pieces and season with salt and pepper. Finely chop the onion and garlic. Slice the courgette. Blanch the tomatoes in boiling water for 1–2 minutes. Drain, rinse in cold water and skin them. Chop the tomato flesh.

2. Put the onion, garlic, courgettes and tomatoes into a microwave-proof dish. Cover and cook on HIGH, stirring once, for about 5 minutes.

3. Stir in the turkey pieces. Cover and cook on HIGH for a further 4–5 minutes, until the turkey turns an even colour.

4. Meanwhile, remove any thick stalks from the basil and finely chop the leaves. Stir the crème fraîche into the turkey ragoût and adjust the seasoning, if necessary. Sprinkle over the basil and serve at once with boiled rice.

Pork tenderloin in herb sauce

Easy to make

You could also make this dish with veal or chicken.

Serves 2
300 g/11 oz pork tenderloin
1 shallot
¼ bunch fresh chervil
1 bunch fresh parsley
½ bunch fresh basil
15 ml/1 tablespoon dry white wine
120 ml/4 fl oz double cream
salt
freshly ground white pepper
boiled rice, to serve

Approximately per portion:
2,000 kj/480 kcal
30 g protein
38 g fat
4 g carbohydrate

● Approximate preparation
  time: 30 minutes

---

1. Trim the pork and cut into thin strips. Finely chop the shallot.

2. Finely chop the chervil. Pull the parsley and basil leaves off their stalks and finely chop the herbs.

3. Mix together the shallot, chervil, parsley, basil, wine and cream in a microwave-proof dish. Season well with salt and pepper.

4. Cook the herb sauce on HIGH, stirring once, for about 3 minutes, until the herbs have softened.

5. Stir in the pork strips. Cover and cook on HIGH, stirring once, for about 4 minutes, until they turn an even colour.

6. If necessary, season again with salt and pepper. Serve at once with boiled rice.

Tip

Chervil is a delicate herb that resembles flat leaf parsley in appearance. It wilts quickly after picking, so it should be used as soon as possible. Its flavour is also similar to that of parsley, with a slight hint of aniseed. It is an excellent herb for flavouring creamy sauces.

Above: Turkey ragoût with tomatoes and courgettes
Below: Pork tenderloin in herb sauce

Ratatouille

Speciality from Provence in southern France

Serves 3–4
2 small aubergines
300 g/11 oz baby courgettes
300 g/11 oz mixed peppers
300 g/11 oz tomatoes
1 large onion
2 garlic cloves
1 fresh rosemary sprig
1 fresh sage sprig
1 fresh thyme sprig
45 ml/3 tablespoons olive oil
1 bay leaf
salt
freshly ground white pepper
pinch of sugar
boiled new potatoes and garlic
   bread, to serve

For 3 people, approximately per portion:
710 kj/170 kcal
6 g protein
9 g fat
16 g carbohydrate

● Approximate preparation
   time: 45 minutes

I. Dice the aubergines. Slice the courgettes. Core and seed the peppers and cut the flesh into matchstick strips. Blanch the tomatoes in boiling water for 1–2 minutes, drain, rinse in cold water and skin them. Finely dice the tomato flesh. Thinly slice the onion and push out into rings. Finely chop the garlic. Coarsely chop the rosemary and sage. Pull the thyme leaves off their stalks.

2. Put the aubergines and the oil into a large microwave-proof dish. Cook on HIGH, stirring once, for about 3 minutes.

3. Add the courgettes, peppers, tomatoes, onion, garlic, rosemary, sage, thyme and bay leaf.

4. Season the ratatouille with salt, pepper and sugar to taste. Cover and cook on HIGH, stirring twice, for about 12 minutes, until the vegetables are tender, but still firm to the bite. Remove the dish from the oven and leave the vegetables to stand for 2–3 minutes, then remove the bay leaf. Serve with new potatoes and garlic bread.

Tip

To make garlic bread, thickly slice a small French loaf, without cutting right through. Mash together 115 g/4 oz butter, 3 crushed garlic cloves and 5 ml/1 teaspoon finely chopped fresh parsley. Spread the butter between the slices. Wrap in kitchen paper and cook on HIGH for 1–1½ minutes.

Cauliflower with ham and herbs

Easy to make • Good value

Serves 2–3
1 medium cauliflower
75 ml/5 tablespoons water
salt
115 g/4 oz boiled ham
1 tomato
½ bunch fresh parsley
½ bunch fresh dill
½ bunch fresh chives
105 ml/7 tablespoons crème fraîche
freshly ground white pepper

For 2 people, approximately per portion:
1,500 kj/360 kcal
22 g protein
24 g fat
15 g carbohydrate

● Approximate preparation
   time: 30 minutes

I. Cut the cauliflower into individual florets.

2. Put the cauliflower, water and a pinch of salt into a microwave-proof dish. Cover and cook on HIGH for about 10 minutes.

3. Meanwhile, trim any fat from the ham and dice the meat. Blanch the tomato in boiling water for 1–2 minutes drain, rinse in cold water and skin. Finely chop the tomato flesh. Remove the thick stems from the parsley, dill and chives and finely chop the leaves.

4. Mix together the ham, tomato, parsley, dill, chives and crème fraîche and season well with salt and pepper.

5. Drain the cauliflower and return to the dish. Stir in the ham cream. Cover and cook on HIGH for a further 2 minutes, until the vegetables are tender, but still firm to the bite.

Above: Ratatouille
Below: Cauliflower with ham and herbs

Asparagus with herb butter

Easy to make

Asparagus remains very aromatic in the microwave because it can be cooked in a short time without much liquid. However, the microwave is not suitable for cooking a large quantity of asparagus because the cooking time then becomes too long.

Serves 2–3
750 g/1 lb 10 oz green asparagus
pinch of sugar
salt
175 ml/6 fl oz water

For the herb butter:
½ bunch fresh parsley
½ bunch fresh basil
1 garlic clove
115 g/4 oz softened butter
7.5 ml/1½ teaspoons lemon juice
2.5 ml/½ teaspoon English or
  Dijon mustard

For 2 people, approximately per portion:
1,700 kj/400 kcal
8 g protein
42 g fat
7 g carbohydrate

● Approximate preparation time: 35 minutes

1. To make the herb butter, remove the thick stalks from the parsley and basil and finely chop the leaves. Crush the garlic.

2. Cream the butter with a fork and beat in the parsley, basil, garlic, lemon juice and mustard until thoroughly incorporated. Form the herb butter into a roll, wrap in aluminium foil and set aside in the refrigerator until you are ready to serve the asparagus.

3. Trim the asparagus and thinly peel the thicker bottom ends of the stalks with a vegetable peeler.

4. Arrange the asparagus in the base of a large microwave-proof dish. Mix sugar and salt to taste with the water and pour it over the asparagus.

5. Cover and cook on HIGH for about 13 minutes, until it is tender but still firm to the bite. Halfway through the cooking time move the stalks on the outside to the middle of the dish and those in the middle to the outside.

6. Carefully lift the asparagus out of the cooking liquid, drain and transfer to individual warmed serving plates. Unwrap the herb butter and cut into slices. Serve the asparagus and hand the herb butter separately.

Tip

When buying asparagus, look for even-coloured spears with tight buds. The spears can vary from very thin to really plump, but avoid long, pale fibrous stems as you will have to discard a large part of them. You should cook and eat asparagus as soon as possible after buying it. It is best served warm, rather than hot.

Peas in cheese sauce

Easy to make

Serves 3
3–4 fresh lemon balm leaves
3–4 fresh tarragon leaves
40g/1½ oz Parmesan cheese
105 ml/7 tablespoons double cream
salt
freshly ground white pepper
300 g/11 oz frozen peas

Approximately per portion:
930 kj/220 kcal
11 g protein
14 g fat
12 g carbohydrate

● Approximate preparation time: 20 minutes

1. Finely chop the lemon balm and tarragon leaves. Grate the Parmesan cheese.

2. Mix together the lemon balm, tarragon, cheese and cream in a microwave-proof dish. Season with salt and pepper to taste.

3. Cook the cream mixture on MEDIUM for about 2 minutes, until the cheese has melted.

4. Stir in the peas, cover and cook on HIGH, stirring once, for about 6 minutes, until the peas are tender, but still firm to the bite

Above: Asparagus with herb butter
Below: Peas in cheese sauce

Artichokes with herb dip

Easy to make

Serves 2
2 artichokes
   (each about 250 g/9 oz)
120 ml/4 fl oz water
15 ml/1 tablespoon lemon juice
salt

For the dip:
150 ml/¼ pint crème fraîche
2.5 ml/½ teaspoon English mustard
5 ml/1 teaspoon olive oil
7.5 ml/1½ teaspoons lemon juice
1 garlic clove
½ bunch fresh parsley
½ bunch fresh dill
½ bunch fresh chives
freshly ground white pepper

Approximately per portion:
1,600 kj/380 kcal
9 g protein
26 g fat
5 g carbohydrate

● Approximate preparation
   time: 30 minutes

---

1. Trim the artichoke stalks. Mix together the water, lemon juice and a pinch of salt in a microwave-proof dish. Add the artichokes.

2. Cover and cook on HIGH, turning the artichokes once, for about 14 minutes. The artichokes are cooked when the leaves can be pulled off easily. Drain.

3. Meanwhile, make the dip. Mix together the crème fraîche,

mustard, oil and lemon juice. Crush the garlic. Remove the thick stalks from the parsley and finely chop the leaves. Finely chop the dill. Snip the chives. Mix the garlic, parsley, dill and chives into the dip.

4. Season the dip well with salt and pepper. Serve the artichokes and hand the dip separately.

Creamy mushrooms

Easy to make

As well as button and oyster mushrooms, this recipe also works well with shiitake mushrooms. Instead of fresh mushrooms, you could also use dried ones, such as bay boletus. You will need about 40 g/1½ oz dried mushrooms.

Serves 2
½ bunch fresh parsley
3–4 fresh sage leaves
1 small onion
1 garlic clove
400 g/14 oz button or
   oyster mushrooms
15 ml/1 tablespoon lemon juice
15 g/½ oz butter
salt
freshly ground white pepper
30 ml/2 tablespoons crème fraîche

Approximately per portion:
380 kj/90 kcal
6 g protein
6 g fat
4 g carbohydrate

● Approximate preparation
   time: 30 minutes

---

1. Pull the parsley leaves off their stalks and chop finely. Finely chop the sage leaves. Finely chop the onion and garlic.

2. Thinly slice the button mushrooms or tear the oyster mushrooms into pieces. Mix the mushrooms with the lemon juice, to prevent discolouration.

3. Put the onion, garlic and butter into a microwave-proof dish. Cook on HIGH for about 2 minutes. Stir in the mushrooms, parsley and sage and season to taste with salt and pepper.

4. Cook on HIGH, stirring once, for about 4 minutes. Stir in the crème fraîche and cook on HIGH for a further 1 minute. Serve the mushrooms immediately.

Tip

If you have bought too many mushrooms, you can dry them in the microwave. Slice the mushrooms and spread them out on kitchen paper. Dry them in the microwave on HIGH, turning once, for about 3 minutes.

Above: Creamy mushrooms
Below: Artichokes with herb dip

Napkin loaf

For guests

This unusual loaf tastes best with meat dishes with a strong sauce.

Serves 4
1 stick of French bread (250 g/9 oz)
25 g/1 oz butter
3 eggs
300 g/11 oz flour
salt
about 350 ml/12 fl oz milk
1 bunch fresh parsley

Approximately per portion:
2,700 kj/640 kcal
26 g protein
21 g fat
91 g carbohydrate

● Approximate preparation time: 1½ hours

  (1 hour resting time)

1. Finely dice the bread and divide into 2 portions in microwave-proof dishes. Add half the butter to each portion and heat each on HIGH, stirring once, for about 3 minutes.

2. Set the bread aside to cool. Separate the eggs and reserve the whites. Sift the flour with a pinch of salt into a mixing bowl. Add the egg yolks and enough milk to make a smooth dough. Mix thoroughly. Cover the dough and set aside to rest for 1 hour.

3. Remove the thick stalks from the parsley and finely chop the leaves. Beat the egg whites with a pinch of salt until they form stiff peaks. Fold the egg whites and parsley into the diced bread, then carefully mix with the dough.

4. Soak a clean tea cloth or napkin in cold water and wring out well. Put the dough into the middle of the cloth and form into a roll. Roll it out gently inside the cloth. Do not be too firm, as the dough stretches during cooking.

5. Fasten the cloth at both ends with string and put it on a microwave-proof plate. Cook on MEDIUM for about 10 minutes. Turn it over halfway through the cooking time.

6. Carefully remove the loaf from the cloth and cut into slices. Transfer the slices to warmed plates and serve.

Dumplings

Easy to make

These simple, but delicious dumplings go extremely well with roasts, mushrooms in cream sauce and sauerkraut. They are a German speciality

Serves 4
5 day-old rolls
about 250 ml/8 fl oz milk
1 onion
1 bunch fresh parsley
1 egg
1 egg yolk
salt
15–30 ml/1–2 tablespoons white
  breadcrumbs (optional)

Approximately per portion:
1,100 kj/260 kcal
11 g protein
8 g fat
35 g carbohydrate

● Approximate preparation time: 40 minutes

1. Cut the rolls into thin slices and put them into a bowl.

2. Pour the milk into a microwave-proof bowl and heat on HIGH for about 3 minutes.

3. Pour the hot milk over the sliced rolls. Put another bowl on top of the sliced rolls to weigh them down and set aside for about 10 minutes.

4. Finely chop the onion. Remove the thick stalks from the parsley and finely chop the leaves.

5. Add the onion, parsley, egg and egg yolk to the soaked rolls. Season the mixture with salt to taste and knead thoroughly until it forms a workable dough. If the dough is too wet, mix in some additional breadcrumbs.

6. Shape the dough into small dumplings in the palms of your hands and arrange them on a microwave-proof plate.

7. Cook the dumplings on HIGH for about 8 minutes. Turn them over halfway through the cooking time.

Above: Napkin loaf
Below: Dumplings

Potatoes in their skins

Easy to make • Quick

Baking potatoes in the microwave not only saves time, but is also very economic and 'green' because the cooking time is so much shorter than baking in a conventional oven.

400 g/14 oz small potatoes of equal size

Approximately per portion:
590 kj/140 kcal
4 g protein
0 g fat
31 g carbohydrate

● Approximate preparation time: 15 minutes

---

1. Scrub the potatoes well under cold running water.

2. Pierce the skins all over several times with a fork. This is important to prevent their bursting during cooking.

3. Put the potatoes into a large microwave-proof dish in a single layer. Cover and cook on HIGH for about 8 minutes, until they are soft, but not disintegrating.

4. Leave to stand for 2–3 minutes, then serve.

Variation
You can also prepare boiled potatoes in the same way in the microwave oven. Peel and dice the potatoes. Put them in a microwave-proof dish, together with 30 ml/2 tablespoons water and a pinch of salt. Cook on HIGH for about 8 minutes.

Tip

If you want to change the quantity, remember that double the quantity requires double the time. However, if the quantity is too large, it is no longer worth cooking in the microwave.

Mashed potatoes

Good value

Serves 2
400 g/14 oz floury potatoes
30 ml/2 tablespoons water
120 ml/4 fl oz milk
10 g/¼ oz butter
salt

For the garnish:
25 g/1 oz butter
30 ml/2 tablespoons fresh white breadcrumbs
30 ml/2 tablespoons finely chopped fresh parsley

Approximately per portion:
920 kj/220 kcal
6 g protein
7 g fat
34 g carbohydrate

● Approximate preparation time: 20 minutes

---

1. Cut the potatoes into fairly small pieces

2. Put the potatoes and water into a microwave-proof dish. Cover and cook on HIGH for about 8 minutes, until they are soft.

3. Drain the potatoes, cover and set aside.

4. Put the milk into a microwave-proof bowl and heat on HIGH for about 2 minutes, until it is very hot. Leave to stand for 1–2 minutes to prevent delayed boiling (see page 7).

5. Mash the potatoes with a fork or a potato masher. Beat in the milk and butter and season to taste with salt.

6. To make the garnish, put the butter in a microwave-proof bowl and melt on HIGH for 30 seconds. Stir in the breadcrumbs and cook on HIGH, stirring once, for 1 minute. Stir in the parsley. Sprinkle over the mashed potato and serve.

Tip

You can grill potatoes quickly in a combination microwave. Peel or scrub 400 g/14 oz potatoes. Cut them into slices or in half lengthways. Put the potatoes into the microwave grill pan and drizzle over a little vegetable oil. Grill on MEDIUM for about 12 minutes, until they are soft and browned on top. Sprinkle with a little salt and serve.

Above: Potatoes in their skins
Below: Mashed potatoes

Hollandaise sauce

For guests • Easy to make

Serves 4
150 g/5 oz butter
3 egg yolks
45 ml/3 tablespoons lukewarm water
15 ml/1 tablespoon lemon juice
salt
freshly ground white pepper

Approximately per portion:
1,300 kj/310 kcal
2 g protein
34 g fat
0 g carbohydrate

● Approximate preparation
time: 10 minutes

Variation
A Béarnaise sauce is made in a
similar way. Finely chop 2 shallots.
Pull the leaves off the stalks of
4 sprigs fresh tarragon and 4 sprigs
fresh chervil. Finely chop the leaves
and put them in a microwave
proof bowl, together with the
shallots, 50 ml/2 fl oz white wine
and 45 ml/3 tablespoons white
wine vinegar. Heat on HIGH for
about 6 minutes, until the liquid
has reduced to about 15 ml/
1 tablespoon. Strain and reserve
the liquid. Make the sauce in the
same way as the Hollandaise
sauce, substituting the reserved
liquid for 15 ml/1 tablespoon of
the water and cayenne pepper for
the white pepper.

1. Put the butter into a
microwave-proof dish. Heat it on
HIGH for about 1½ minutes, until
it has melted.

2. Meanwhile, in a microwave-
proof dish beat the egg yolks with
the water until they are foamy.

3. Gradually add the melted butter
in a thin stream, stirring constantly.

4. Cook on MEDIUM for about
2 minutes, until thickened. Then
beat the sauce thoroughly with a
whisk, beating in the lemon juice.
Season the sauce to taste with salt
and pepper.

Béchamel sauce

Good value

Béchamel sauce tastes good with vegetables, such as salsify and asparagus. It is also a favourite ingredient for many oven-baked dishes, such as a classic lasagne.

Serves 4
65 g/2½ oz butter
65 g/2½ oz flour
750 ml/1¼ pints milk
salt
freshly grated nutmeg

Approximately per portion:
1,200 kj/290 kcal
8 g protein
19 g fat
20 g carbohydrate

● Approximate preparation time: 15 minutes

1. Put the butter into a microwave-proof dish and heat on HIGH for about 1½ minutes, until it has melted.

2. Stir in the flour and cook on HIGH for a further 2 minutes.

3. Stir in the milk. Cook on HIGH, stirring well once, for about 7 minutes, until thickened. Be careful of delayed boiling (see page 7).

4. Season the béchamel sauce with salt and nutmeg to taste.

Red fruit compôte with vanilla sauce

Exquisite • For guests

If you cannot obtain fresh mixed soft fruits, you can use frozen and thawed fruits instead.

Serves 4
For the compôte:
600 g/1 lb 5 oz mixed fresh soft
fruit, such as raspberries,
redcurrants, loganberries,
strawberries, blackberries
120 ml/4 fl oz dry, fruity red wine
60 ml/4 tablespoons cornflour
120 ml/4 fl oz unsweetened
fruit juice
50 g/2 oz sugar
grated rind of ½ lemon

For the sauce:
400 ml/14 fl oz milk
1 vanilla pod
10 ml/2 teaspoons cornflour
2 eggs
25 g/1 oz caster sugar

Approximately per portion:
1,500 kj/360 kcal
12 g protein
10 g fat
50 g carbohydrate

● Approximate preparation
time: 1 hour

---

1. To make the compôte, pick over but do not wash the raspberries. Wash the other fruits. Pull the redcurrants off their stalks, cut up the strawberries and leave the blackberries whole.

2. In a small bowl stir together 45 ml/3 tablespoons of the wine and the cornflour to make a smooth paste. Mix together the remaining wine, the fruit juice, sugar and lemon rind and put into a microwave-proof dish. Cover and heat on HIGH for about 3 minutes.

3. Stir the cornflour paste, then stir it into the wine and fruit juice mixture. Cook on HIGH for a further 2 minutes. Beat well with a whisk halfway through the cooking time and again at the end of the cooking time.

4. Gently mix in the soft fruits and cook on HIGH for a further 1 minute, until the mixture has thickened slightly.

5. Pour the compôte into 4 individual serving bowls or a large serving dish and set aside to cool.

6. Make the sauce. Reserve 30 ml/ 2 tablespoons of the milk and pour the remainder into a microwave-proof bowl. Slit the vanilla pod lengthways with a sharp knife. Scrape out the pulp and add to the milk, together with the pod. Cover and heat on HIGH for about 4 minutes.

7. Meanwhile, mix together the cornflour and the reserved milk. Separate the eggs.

8. Beat together the egg yolks, sugar and cornflour paste.

9. Beat the egg mixture into the milk with a whisk. Cook on HIGH, stirring once, for about 3 minutes, until thickened.

10. Remove the vanilla pod from the bowl. Stir the sauce thoroughly and set aside to cool slightly. Beat the egg whites until stiff, then fold into the sauce.

11. Set aside to cool completely, stirring from time to time to prevent a skin forming. Serve the compôte and hand the vanilla sauce separately.

Fruity red compôte with creamy vanilla sauce melts in the mouth.

Chocolate pudding

Easy to make

Serves 4
3 eggs
40 g/1½ oz butter, plus extra
    for greasing
20 g/¾ oz sugar
50 g/2 oz ground almonds
90 g/3½ oz plain chocolate, grated
pinch of salt
grated rind of ¼ lemon
60–90 ml/4–6 tablespoons
    breadcrumbs
150 ml/¼ pint double cream
7.5 ml/1½ teaspoons vanilla sugar
20 ml/4 teaspoons grated chocolate
    (optional), to decorate

Approximately per portion:
2,100 kj/500 kcal
14 g protein
42 g fat
20 g carbohydrate

● Approximate preparation
  time: 25 minutes

---

1. Separate the eggs and reserve the whites. Beat together the egg yolks, butter and sugar until the mixture is foamy. Beat the egg whites until stiff and fold into the egg yolk mixture. Sprinkle over the almonds, chocolate, salt and lemon rind and mix gently but thoroughly.

2. Butter 4 individual microwave-proof bowls or moulds and scatter breadcrumbs over the butter. Divide the chocolate mixture between the bowls, so that they are about two-thirds full.

3. Cook on MEDIUM for about 5 minutes, until the mixture has just set.

4. Leave the bowls to stand for 3–4 minutes. Meanwhile, beat the cream, together with the vanilla sugar. Carefully tip the puddings out on to individual serving plates, spoon over or pipe a swirl of the vanilla-flavoured cream and decorate with grated chocolate, if liked. Serve immediately.

Quick orange cream

Easy to make • For guests

Serves 4
2 oranges
105 ml/7 tablespoons water
105 ml/7 tablespoons sparkling
    white wine
2 eggs
90 g/3½ oz caster sugar
25 g/1 oz cornflour
salt
105 ml/7 tablespoons double cream
4 fresh lemon balm sprigs,
    to decorate

Approximately per portion:
1,400 kj/ 330 kcal
9 g protein
14 g fat
36 g carbohydrate

● Approximate preparation
  time: 1½ hours (1 hour
  cooling time)

---

1. Finely grate the rind of 1 orange. Squeeze the juice from both oranges.

2. Mix together the orange rind, orange juice, water and wine in a microwave-proof bowl. Separate the eggs and reserve the whites. Add the egg yolks, sugar and cornflour to the orange juice mixture and beat thoroughly with a balloon whisk.

3. Cook the mixture on MEDIUM, beating twice with a whisk, for about 8 minutes, until thickened.

4. Set aside to cool slightly. Beat the egg whites with a pinch of salt until they form stiff peaks. Beat the cream until stiff. Fold the egg whites and the cream into the orange mixture.

5. Divide the orange cream between 4 individual serving dishes and set aside to cool for about 1 hour. Decorate with the lemon balm leaves and serve.

Above: Chocolate pudding
Below: Quick orange cream

Vanilla moulds with peach sauce

Exquisite • For guests

This creamy pudding from Italy is very easy to make.

Serves 4
1 vanilla pod
500 ml/17 fl oz double cream
40 g/1½ oz caster sugar
120 ml/4 fl oz water
1 sachet gelatine

For the peach sauce:
4 peaches
50 ml/2 fl oz dry white wine
5–10 ml/1–2 teaspoons caster sugar (optional)

Approximately per portion:
2,000 kj/480 kcal
5 g protein
40 g fat
25 g carbohydrate

● Approximate preparation time: 6½ hours (about 6 hours cooling time)

Tip

Strawberry sauce is also delicious with vanilla moulds. You need about 400 g/14 oz strawberries, which are then prepared in the same way as the peach sauce.

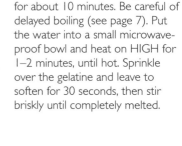

1. Slit the vanilla pod lengthways with a sharp, pointed knife. Scrape out the pulp and put it, together with the pod, into a high-sided, microwave-proof bowl. Add the cream and sugar and mix well.

2. Cook on HIGH, stirring twice, for about 10 minutes. Be careful of delayed boiling (see page 7). Put the water into a small microwave-proof bowl and heat on HIGH for 1–2 minutes, until hot. Sprinkle over the gelatine and leave to soften for 30 seconds, then stir briskly until completely melted.

3. Remove the vanilla pod from the cream. Pour the gelatine into the cream in a single, continuous stream, stirring constantly. Rinse 4 cups or individual moulds with cold water and divide the cream between them. Set aside in the refrigerator for 6 hours until the moulds have set.

4. Peel and stone the peaches. Put the peaches and wine in a food processor and work to make a smooth purée. Stir in sugar, if necessary. Loosen the moulds by running a knife blade around the edges. Tip on to individual serving plates, pour the peach sauce over and beside them and serve.

Curd cheese dumplings with strawberry sauce

Exquisite • Good value

Serves 3–4
For the sauce:
350 g/12 oz strawberries
15 ml/1 tablespoon caster sugar
50 ml/2 fl oz double cream

For the dumplings:
1 vanilla pod
150 g/5 oz curd cheese
30 ml/2 tablespoons caster sugar
10 ml/2 teaspoons lemon juice
1 egg
1 egg yolk
25 g/1 oz flour
30–45 ml/2–3 tablespoons
*   breadcrumbs*

For 3 people, approximately per portion:
1,300 kj/310 kcal
13 g protein
16 g fat
30 g carbohydrate

● Approximate preparation
   time: 30 minutes

1. First make the sauce. reserve 4 strawberries for the garnish and mash the remainder with a fork. Mix together the strawberries, sugar and cream. Cover and set aside in the refrigerator until you are ready to serve the dumplings.

2. To make the dumplings, slit the vanilla pod with a sharp, pointed knife. Scrape out the pulp into a bowl. Add the curd cheese, sugar, lemon juice, egg, egg yolk and flour and mix together. Add enough breadcrumbs to turn the mixture into a workable dough.

3. Using 2 teaspoons, shape little dumplings from the dough and arrange them on 2 microwave-proof plates. Cook, one plate at a time, on HIGH for about 3½ minutes.

4. Divide the dumplings between 4 individual serving plates. Stir the strawberry sauce thoroughly and spoon a little on to each plate. Garnish with reserved strawberries and serve, handing the remaining sauce separately.

Stuffed roast chicken

Easy to make

Serves 4
1 x 1.4 kg/2½ lb chicken,
   with giblets
1 day-old roll
2 spring onions
115 g/4 oz button mushrooms
15 ml/1 tablespoon lemon juice
4–6 fresh marjoram leaves
40 g/1½ oz butter
salt
freshly ground white pepper

Approximately per portion:
2,400 kj/570 kcal
74 g protein
29 g fat
7 g carbohydrate

● Approximate preparation
   time: 1 hour 10 minutes

---

1. Remove the giblets from the chicken. Trim and finely chop the heart and liver. Discard the neck.

2. To make the stuffing, place the roll in a small bowl, cover with lukewarm water and set aside to

soak for about 10 minutes, until soft. Finely chop the spring onions. Slice the mushrooms. Mix together the mushrooms, and lemon juice. Finely chop the marjoram.

3. Squeeze the excess water from the roll and crumble it. Mix together the crumbled roll, spring onions, mushrooms, marjoram, chicken heart and liver and half the butter.

4. Put the remaining butter into a small microwave-proof bowl and heat on HIGH for about 30 seconds, until melted.

5. Rub salt and pepper on to the inside and outside of the chicken. Season the mushroom stuffing with salt and pepper to taste and spoon it into the chicken.

6. Secure the opening with trussing thread. Lay the chicken, breast side down, on the microwave shelf. Baste it with some of the melted butter and put it into the middle of the microwave.

7. Roast the chicken for about 35 minutes on MEDIUM and circulating air at 180°C/350°F (with over- and under-heat at 200°C/400°F) until it is crisp and golden. Turn the chicken over half way through the cooking time and baste it with the remaining melted butter.

8. Wrap the roast chicken in aluminium foil and let it stand for about 5 minutes. Then, remove the trussing thread and cut the chicken into 8 pieces, arrange them on warmed plates and serve.

Tip

Poultry cooks particularly well in combination microwaves. For example, try grilled breast of duck. It only takes about 11 minutes on MEDIUM and a medium grill setting. Grill the breast with the skin side up and turn it over after about 9 minutes.

Stuffed chicken cooks particularly well in a combination microwave. It turns crispy brown in the circulating air or over-and-under-heat.

Osso buco

Speciality from Italy

Serves 2
2 carrots
1 celery stick
200 g/7 oz tomatoes
1 onion
1 garlic clove
1 bunch fresh parsley
25 g/1 oz butter
2 x 4 cm/1½ inch thick slices
    knuckle of veal (osso buco)
50 ml/2 fl oz water
salt
freshly ground white pepper

For the garnish:
rind of 1 lemon
1 garlic clove
½ bunch fresh parsley

Approximately per portion:
1,700 kj/400 kcal
56 g protein
15 g fat
11 g carbohydrate

● Approximate preparation
   time: 1 hour

---

1. Finely chop the carrots and celery. Blanch the tomatoes in boiling water for 1–2 minutes, drain, rinse under cold water and skin. Dice the tomato flesh. Finely chop the onion and garlic. Finely chop the parsley.

2. Put the carrots, celery, onion, garlic, parsley and butter into a large microwave-proof dish. Cook on HIGH, stirring once or twice, for about 6 minutes.

3. Add the veal. Mix the tomatoes with the water, season to taste with salt and pepper and pour over the meat. Cover and cook on LOW and circulating air at 200°C/400°F (over-and-under-heat 220°C/425°F) for about 40 minutes. Turn the meat once during the cooking time and, if necessary, add a little hot water.

4. Meanwhile prepare the garnish. Finely chop the lemon rind, garlic and parsley. Mix them together. Leave the meat to stand for 5 minutes, then scatter over the garnish and serve.

Grilled lamb

Easy to make

Serves 2
2 garlic cloves
1 fresh rosemary sprig
2 cm/¾ inch long strip thinly pared
    lemon rind
juice of ½ lemon
30 ml/2 tablespoons olive oil
freshly ground white pepper
250 g/9 oz boneless leg of lamb
salt
boiled potatoes and French beans
    cooked with lardons, to serve

Approximately per portion:
1,500 kj/360 kcal
23 g protein
30 g fat
1 g carbohydrate

● Approximate preparation
   time: 4½ hours (4 hours
   marinating time)

---

1. Finely chop the garlic, together with the lemon rind. Coarsely chop the rosemary.

2. Mix together the garlic, rosemary, lemon rind, lemon juice and olive oil and season well with pepper. Lay the lamb into a deep dish and pour over the marinade. Set aside in the refrigerator to marinate for about 4 hours, turning it over once or twice.

3. Put the lamb, together with the marinade, into a microwave-proof dish. Put the dish on the shelf in the middle of the microwave. Grill on MEDIUM and medium grill setting for about 15 minutes. Turn the meat over after about 9 minutes.

4. Leave the meat to stand for 5 minutes, then cut into slices, season with salt and pepper to taste and serve with lied potatoes and French beans.

Above: Grilled lamb
Below: Osso buco

Potato and mushroom gratin

Serves 2–3
300 g/11 oz mushrooms
15 ml/1 tablespoon lemon juice
500 g/1¼ lb floury potatoes, such
*   as Désirée or Maris Piper*
½ bunch fresh thyme or 5 ml/
*   1 teaspoon dried thyme*
salt
freshly ground white pepper
200 ml/7 fl oz double cream
150 g/5 oz mozzarella cheese

For 2 people, approximately per portion:
2,900 kj/690 kcal
27 g protein
45 g fat
43 g carbohydrate

● Approximate preparation
time: 1 hour

---

1. Thinly slice the mushrooms and sprinkle over the lemon juice.

2. Thinly slice the potatoes. Strip the fresh thyme leaves from their stalks, if using.

3. Arrange the potatoes and mushrooms in layers in a microwave-proof dish, scattering fresh thyme leaves or sprinkling dried thyme over each layer and seasoning to taste with salt and pepper.

4. Carefully pour in the cream. Dice the cheese and sprinkle over the top of the dish.

5. Put the gratin on the shelf in the middle of the microwave. Cook on MEDIUM with circulating air at 200°C/400°F (over- and-under-heat at 220°C/425°F) for about 25 minutes, until the top is golden brown and the potatoes are soft.

Vegetable quiche

For guests

Makes a 28 cm/11 inch flan
For the dough:
250 g/9 oz plain or wholemeal flour
salt
130 g/4½ oz butter
30 ml/2 tablespoons yogurt

For the filling:
2 leeks
150 g/5 oz mushrooms
15 ml/1 tablespoon lemon juice
1 red pepper
1 yellow pepper
2 garlic cloves
1 bunch fresh parsley
115 g/4 oz Cheddar cheese
3 eggs
105 ml/7 tablespoons double cream
freshly ground black pepper

For 12 slices, approximately per slice:
1,100 kj/260 kcal
10 g protein
17 g fat
18 g carbohydrate

● Approximate preparation
time: 1½ hours

---

1. Sift the flour with a pinch of salt into a mixing bowl. Cut the butter into small pieces and add to the flour, together with the yogurt. Lightly knead to form a smooth, elastic dough. If the dough is too firm, mix in a little cold water.

2. Roll out the pastry and use to line a 28 cm/11 inch loose-based flan tin. Set aside in the refrigerator to rest for about 1 hour.

3. Meanwhile, make the filling. Trim and thinly slice the leeks, including any green parts that are not tough. Cut the mushrooms into quarters and sprinkle over the lemon juice. Core, seed and dice the peppers. Finely chop the garlic. Remove any thick stems from the parsley and finely chop the leaves.

4. Mix together the red and yellow peppers, leeks, garlic, parsley and mushrooms. Grate the cheese. Separate the eggs.

5. Beat together the egg yolks, cheese and cream and add to the vegetable mixture. Whisk the egg whites until they form stiff peaks. Season with pepper and carefully fold into the vegetable mixture. Spoon the mixture evenly over the pastry base.

6. Put the quiche on the shelf of the microwave and bake on LOW for about 30 minutes with circulating air at 190°C/375°F (over- and-under-heat at 200°C/ 400°F), until the quiche is set and the surface is golden brown. Leave the quiche to stand for 5 minutes, then serve.

Above: Vegetable quiche
Below: Potato and mushroom gratin

Rhubarb with crème fraîche topping

For guests

Serves 4
butter, for greasing
700 g/1½ lb rhubarb
90 g/3½ oz sugar
150 ml/¼ pint crème fraîche
15 ml/1 tablespoon clear honey
5 ml/1 teaspoon ground cinnamon
double cream, to serve

Approximately per portion:
940 kj/220 kcal
2 g protein
12 g fat
27 g carbohydrate

● Approximate preparation time: 35 minutes

1. Grease a microwave-proof dish with butter.

2. Chop the rhubarb into small pieces. Mix together the rhubarb and sugar and set aside for about 10 minutes.

3. Drain the rhubarb and put it into the prepared dish. Mix together the crème fraîche, honey and cinnamon and spread it over the rhubarb.

4. Put the dish on the shelf in the middle of the microwave. Cook on MEDIUM for about 10 minutes with a medium grill setting, until the rhubarb is soft and the top is golden. Serve warm with cream.

Peach meringue pie

Easy to make

This melt-in the mouth dessert can also be made with fresh apricots.

Serves 4
600 g/1 lb 5 oz peaches
butter, for greasing
30 ml/2 tablespoons clear honey
30 ml/2 tablespoons lemon juice
15 ml/1 tablespoon amaretto (almond liqueur)
4 egg whites
salt
15 ml/1 tablespoon caster sugar
75 g/3 oz finely ground walnuts

Approximately per portion:
940 kj/220 kcal
5 g protein
12 g fat
24 g carbohydrate

● Approximate preparation time: 40 minutes

1. Pour boiling water over the peaches and set aside for 3–4 minutes. Drain, rinse in cold water and skin. Cut the flesh off the stones into thin slices.

2. Grease a microwave-proof dish with a little butter. Arrange the peach slices, slightly overlapping, in the base of the dish.

3. Put the honey, lemon juice and amaretto into a small microwave-proof bowl and heat on HIGH for 1 minute, until the honey has melted. Stir the honey mixture and pour it over the peaches.

4. Beat the egg whites with a pinch of salt to form stiff peaks. Gradually beat in the sugar. Fold in the walnuts. Spoon the meringue mixture on top of the peaches and spread to cover them completely.

5. Put the dish on the shelf in the middle of the microwave. Cook on MEDIUM for about 10 minutes with a medium grill setting until the meringue is set and golden brown. Set aside to cool slightly and serve the pie lukewarm.

Tip

If the peaches are very ripe, it is easy to remove the skins without blanching. You can prepare the nutty meringue using any other nuts. Try it with hazelnuts, almonds and – especially delicious – with pumpkin seeds.

Above: Rhubarb with crème fraîche topping
Below: Peach meringue pie

Redcurrant tart with nut topping

Easy to make

Makes a 28 cm/11 inch round cake
For the tart base:
250 g/9 oz white or wholemeal flour
salt
130 g/4½ oz butter, diced
grated rind of ½ lemon
5 ml/1 teaspoon vanilla essence
15–30 ml/1–2 tablespoons yogurt
50 g/2 oz caster sugar

For the filling:
600 g/1 lb 5 oz redcurrants
115 g/4 oz hazel nuts
2 eggs
105 ml/7 tablespoons double cream
5 ml/1 teaspoon cocoa powder
90 g/3½ oz sugar
icing sugar, for dusting

For 12 piecest, approximately per piece:
1,300 kj/310 kcal
6 g protein
19 g fat
25 g carbohydrate

● Approximate preparation time: 2 hours (1 hour cooling time)

1. First make the tart base. Sift together the flour, and a pinch of salt into a mixing bowl. Add the butter, lemon rind, vanilla essence, yogurt, and sugar and lightly knead to form a smooth, elastic dough. If the dough is too stiff (which is likely if you are using wholemeal flour), knead in a little more yogurt or cold water.

2. Roll out the dough and use it to line a 28 cm/11 inch microwave-proof springform tin. Set aside to rest for about 1 hour.

3. Meanwhile, make the filling. Strip the redcurrants from their stalks. Grind the hazel nuts.

4. Separate the eggs and reserve the whites. Beat together the egg yolks, cream, cocoa powder, nuts and caster sugar. Beat the egg whites until they form stiff peaks, then carefully fold them into the egg yolk mixture.

5. Spoon the redcurrants over the base of the tart shell. Spoon the egg mixture on top and spread to cover completely.

6. Put the tart on the shelf in the middle of the microwave. Bake on LOW and circulating air at 190°C/375°F (over- and-under-heat at 200°C/400°F) for 30 minutes, until it is firm to the touch and and the top is golden brown.

7. Leave the tart to stand for about 5 minutes. Then carefully remove it from the tin and set aside on a cake rack to cool completely. Dust with icing sugar and serve.

Variation
Of course, you can use different fruits for the tart. Peaches, nectarines, cherries, apricots and apples are all suitable and the tart can be prepared in exactly the same way. You can also use rhubarb. First mix it with 115g/4 oz sugar and set aside for about 10 minutes. Then pour off the surplus liquid and use the rhubarb as in the recipe.

Tip

Wholemeal flour soaks up more liquid than refined flour, so the dough will need more liquid. When it is cooling, wholemeal flour also soaks up more liquid than white flour.

Redcurrant tart with nut topping tastes best when it is freshly baked.

58

CONVERSION TABLES

The recipes in this book are designed for microwaves with a highest setting of 600 watts. If you have an appliance with a higher or lower top setting, you can easily convert the cooking times by using the table below. The table has omitted 650 watt and 720 watt microwaves because the difference between these and a 700 watt appliance is minimal. The table also leaves out microwaves with a top setting of 400 watts, as these are mainly suitable for defrosting and warming, but not so good for cooking.

500 watts	600 watts	700 watts
45 seconds	30 seconds	30 seconds
1¼ minutes	1 minute	1 minute
1¾ minutes	1½ minutes	1¼ minutes
2½ minutes	2 minutes	1¾ minutes
2¾ minutes	2¼ minutes	2 minutes
3 minutes	2½ minutes	2 minutes
3½ minutes	3 minutes	2½ minutes
4½ minutes	4 minutes	3½ minutes
5½ minutes	5 minutes	4½ minutes
6½ minutes	6 minutes	5 minutes
8 minutes	7 minutes	6 minutes
9 minutes	8 minutes	7 minutes
10½ minutes	9 minutes	7½ minutes
11½ minutes	10 minutes	8½ minutes
12½ minutes	11 minutes	9½ minutes
13½ minutes	12 minutes	10 minutes
15 minutes	13 minutes	11 minutes
16 minutes	14 minutes	12 minutes
17 minutes	15 minutes	13 minutes
23 minutes	20 minutes	17 minutes
28 minutes	25 minutes	21 minutes
34 minutes	30 minutes	26 minutes

Warming up already cooked food

As a rule, you should warm food that is already cooked on HIGH. For 250 g/9 oz food you can allow a warming up time of about 2 minutes. Dry food, such as meat or fish coated in breadcrumbs, should always be sprinkled with a few drops of water and be covered, so that it does not dry out. Food that cooks quickly is not very suitable for warming up, as it should usually be eaten immediately it is ready. Examples are thin fish fillets or pasta dishes. Fish becomes dry and pasta turns soft or mushy.

Defrosting common foods

The times given in the table below are for thawing food without also warming it. Delicate foods, such as cream, should only be partially thawed and then set aside at room temperature to thaw completely. Always use the DEFROST setting on the microwave.

There have been a number of warnings recently about the health risks of thawing poultry in the microwave. In any case, the meat is very delicate and should thaw slowly in the refrigerator.

Food	Quantity	Time	Standing time	Remarks
Bread	1 slice	30 sec	4 min	
Bread roll	1	30 sec	5 min	turn over once
Cake	1	1–2 min	5 min	only half-thaw cream cake
Butter	250 g/9 oz	3–4 min	20 min	only half-thaw
Cheese	500 g/1¼ lb	4–5 min	25 min	only half-thaw
Cream	250 ml/9 fl oz	2–3 min	5 min	half-thaw, beat while slightly frozen
Whole fish	500 g/1¼ lb	9–12 min	10 min	turn over once
Fish fillets	300 g/11 oz	6–8 min	10 min	turn over once
Scampi	200 g/7 oz	6–8 min	10 min	turn over once
Whole meat	500 g/1¼ lb	15 min	10 min	turn over once
Minced meat	500 g/1¼ lb	10–13 min	15 min	turn over once
Liquids	250 ml/8 fl oz	9–11 min	–	
Vegetables	300 g/11 oz	4–6 min	10 min	turn over once

Great Little Cook Books
Microwave Cooking

Published originally under the title *Aus der Mikrowave* by Gräfe und Unzer Verlag GmbH, München

© 1992 by Gräfe und Unzer Verlag GmbH, München

English-language edition
© 1998 by Transedition Limited, Oxford, England

This edition published by
Aura Books plc

Translation:
Translate-A-Book, Oxford

Editing:
Linda Doeser

Typesetting:
Organ Graphic, Abingdon

10 9 8 7 6 5 4 3 2 1
Printed in Dubai

ISBN 1 901683 41 9

Important advice

Before you switch on your microwave, you should make yourself thoroughly familiar with the manufacturer's instructions. Please also read the information given on pages 4–7 at the front of this book. Take especial care when heating fluids, as there may be delayed boiling. That is, liquids only start to boil when they have been taken out of the microwave. Be careful not to burn yourself! It is always best to leave the liquid to cool in the microwave for a short while after the specified cooking time has finished.

If you have any questions or are still uncertain about anything, you should ask the manufacturer. New appliances present no health risks, but it is recommended that you have older models checked regularly by a specialist supplier.

Cornelia Schinharl
lives in Munich and has always been interested in cooking. After studying languages she then gained extensive knowledge in the field of nutrition by working with a food journalist. She keeps herself up to date on the development of microwave technology through courses and seminars. Since 1985 she has worked as a freelance editor and writer and has written several cookery books.

Odette Teubner
was taught by her father, the internationally renowned food photographer, Christian Teubner. After that she worked for some months as a fashion photographer. She now works exclusively in the Teubner Studio for Food Photography. In her spare time she is an enthusiastic painter of children's portraits, using her own son as a model.

Kerstin Mosny
studied photography at a college in French-speaking Switzerland. She then worked as an assistant to various photographers, including the food photographer, Jürgen Tapprich, in Zurich. She now works in the Teubner Studio for Food Photography..

Note:
Quantities for all recipes are given in both metric and imperial measures and, if appropriate, in standard measuring spoons. They are not interchangeable, so readers should follow one set or the other.
5 ml = 1 teaspoon
15 ml = 1 tablespoon